Parent's Introduction

Whether your child is a beginning reader, a reluctant reader, or an eager reader, this book offers a fun and easy way to encourage and help your child in reading.

Developed with reading education specialists, *We Both Read* books invite you and your child to take turns reading aloud. You read the left-hand pages of the book, and your child reads the right-hand pages—which have been written at one of six early reading levels. The result is a wonderful new reading experience and faster reading development!

You may find it helpful to read the entire book aloud yourself the first time, then invite your child to participate the second time. As you read, try to make the story come alive by reading with expression. This will help to model good fluency. It will also be helpful to stop at various points to discuss what you are reading. This will help increase your child's understanding of what is being read.

In some books, a few challenging words are introduced in the parent's text, distinguished with **bold** lettering. Pointing out and discussing these words can help to build your child's reading vocabulary. If your child is a beginning reader, it may be helpful to run a finger under the text as each of you reads. Please also notice that a "talking parent" ☺ icon precedes the parent's text, and a "talking child" ☺ icon precedes the child's text.

If your child struggles with a word, you can encourage "sounding it out," but keep in mind that not all words can be sounded out. Your child might pick up clues about a word from the picture, other words in the sentence, or any rhyming patterns. If your child struggles with a word for more than five seconds, it is usually best to simply say the word.

Most of all, remember to praise your child's efforts and keep the reading fun. After you have finished the book, ask a few questions and discuss what you have read together. Rereading this book multiple times may also be helpful for your child.

Try to keep the tips above in mind as you read together, but don't worry about doing everything right. Simply sharing the enjoyment of reading together will increase your child's reading skills and help to start your child off on a lifetime of reading enjoyment!

Zoo Day

A We Both Read® Book: Level 1
Guided Reading (for Right-hand Pages): Level E

Text Copyright © 2012, 2015 by Treasure Bay, Inc.
By Bruce Johnson and Sindy McKay
Illustrations Copyright © 2012 by Meredith Johnson

This book is based in part on a We Read Phonics book, *A Day at the Zoo*, but it has been significantly expanded and adapted for the We Both Read shared-reading format. You may find the We Read Phonics version to be a complementary and helpful companion to this title.

Reading Consultant: Bruce Johnson, M.Ed.

We Both Read® is a trademark of Treasure Bay, Inc.

Published by Treasure Bay, Inc.
P.O. Box 119
Novato, CA 94948 USA

Printed in Malaysia

Library of Congress Catalog Card Number: 2014944094

ISBN: 978-1-60115-274-9

Visit us online at:
WeBothRead.com

PR-11-19

Zoo Day

By Bruce Johnson and Sindy McKay

with illustrations by Meredith Johnson

TREASURE BAY

The sun is out and it's a beautiful day to be outside. What can you do?

You can go to the zoo!

 You might start by visiting some big animals, like giraffes and **polar bears**. Giraffes don't mind when it's hot outside.

👓 **Polar bears** like it to be cold.

A hippopotamus is sometimes **called** a **hippo**. A **hippo** has very little hair on its body. To protect its bare skin from the hot sun, it spends much of its time in the water.

A mother **hippo** is **called** a *cow*. A baby is **called** a *pup*.

The biggest animal in the zoo is the African elephant. It is the largest land animal on Earth. It has very large ears. This zoo also has some **smaller** Asian elephants.

They are **smaller** in size and have **smaller** ears.

As you walk through the zoo, you might hear a loud roar. That could mean you're getting close to the **lion** enclosure. A **lion**'s roar can be heard from five miles away!

Lions are very big. Tigers are even bigger!

Lions, tigers, and panthers are often called the "big cats." There may also be some smaller types of wild cats in the zoo. One smaller cat is the **serval**.

It has big ears and long legs. These help the **serval** to hunt.

Be sure to visit the giant panda exhibit, where you can watch pandas eat. Giant pandas spend about 12 hours a day eating **bamboo** shoots, stems, and leaves.

Some people eat **bamboo** too. Do you?

People often call chimps the "clowns of the zoo." They seem to enjoy goofing around and **smiling** for the camera.

This chimp has a big **smile**!

 Some zoos have a special house just for birds called an *aviary*. The roof is very high to give the birds plenty of room to fly.

Most birds can fly. Some birds can also swim.

There are over ten thousand bird species, from tiny hummingbirds to giant ostriches. A zoo can't house them all.

This zoo has a pair of pretty cockatoos. It also has a hawk.

This hawk is on the lookout. What do you think it sees?

Visiting an exhibit of **insects**, spiders, and scorpions can be creepy and fun. Many **insects** protect themselves from predators by blending into their surroundings.

This **insect** looks like a stick. Can you find it?

Scorpions are in the same animal class as **spiders**. A scorpion has a stinger in its tail that injects venom into its prey.

An insect has six legs. A **spider** has eight legs.

The **reptile** area has critters that crawl and coil and creep. Some **reptiles**, like this monitor lizard, stay hot in one spot.

Some **reptiles** stay cool
in a pool.

Crocodiles, alligators, turtles, snakes, and lizards are all reptiles. Some kids are afraid of them.

Some kids love them!

This zoo has animals from the sea too. This is a manatee, sometimes called a "sea cow." In the pool next door are sea lions and seals. They make a loud barking **sound**.

Seals bark, but they do not **sound** like dogs.

　　There is a great variety of animals in the zoo. This zoo has two different kinds of **penguins**. These little guys are rockhopper **penguins**. They are only about one and a half feet tall.

These are king **penguins**. They can grow to be three feet tall.

You might be able to visit a special area where you can pet some of the animals. Here you may find sheep, llamas, goats, and other tame animals.

 You can also feed the animals. Yum, yum!

Taking care of so many animals is a big job! It takes many **zookeepers** to keep them all well fed and to clean their habitats.

The **zookeepers** clean the animals too.

There are also zoo veterinarians who help keep the animals **healthy** and strong. The vets must take care of the animals' teeth and gums.

Vets help all of the animals in the zoo to stay **healthy**. Baby animals often need extra care.

The zoo is a fun place to see animals and learn many things about them too. So the next time you want to **spend** a day outside, why not go and visit the animals?

It is fun to **spend** a day at the zoo!

Glossary

exhibit
to show or display for people to see

predator
an animal that hunts other animals for food

prey
an animal that is hunted by another animal
for food

species
a group of animals or plants that are similar

veterinarian
a doctor for animals

zoo
a place that keeps and cares for wild animals, so
people can see them and learn more about them

zookeeper
a worker who takes care of animals in a zoo

Discussion Questions

Add to the benefits of reading this book by discussing answers to these questions. If needed, you can refer back to pages in the book to help with the answers. Also consider discussing a few of your own questions.

1 If you went to a zoo, what kinds of animals would you like to see there?

2 What is your favorite zoo animal? What are some things you like about it?

3 How are all zoo animals the same? How are some animals different from other animals?

4 What do you think zookeepers do for animals at the zoo?

5 What are some things you think veterinarians might do at the zoo?

If you liked *Zoo Day*, here are some other
We Both Read books you are sure to enjoy!

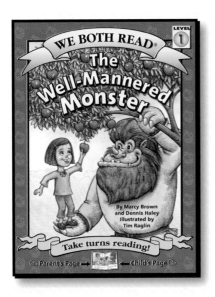

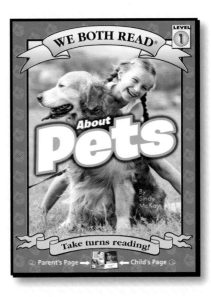

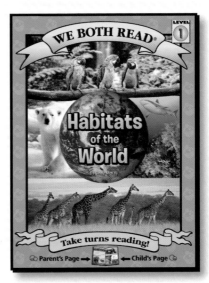

To see all the We Both Read books that are available,
just go online to **WeBothRead.com**.